MW00780508

This book belongs to

_____

I R*ode

Atlanta's Favorite Christmas Tradition

Foreword by Ludlow Porch

Hill Street Press ● Athens, Georgia
Published with Rich's-Macy's

A HILL STREET PRESS BOOK

Published in the United States of America by
Hill Street Press LLC
191 East Broad Street, Suite 209
Athens, Georgia 30601-2848 USA   706-613-7200

The recipes in this book require careful preparation as well as the use of proper ingredients. Neither the publisher nor Rich's-Macy's assumes any liability. • Our best efforts have been used to obtain proper copyright clearance and credit for each of the images in this book. If an unavoidable and inadvertent credit error has occurred it will be corrected in future editions upon notification.

No material in this book may be reproduced, scanned, stored, or transmitted in any form without the prior written consent of the publisher.

Foreword copyright © 2004 by Ludlow Porch.
Copyright © 2004 by Rich's-Macys. All rights reserved.
Text and cover design by Anne Richmond Boston.

Printed in Canada.

Library of Congress Cataloging-in-Publication Data

I rode the pink pig: Atlanta's favorite Christmas tradition.
    p.   cm.
  ISBN 1-58818-099-9 (alk. paper)
  1. Christmas—Georgia—Atlanta—History. 2. Rich's-Macy's (Department store)—History. 3. Amusement rides—Georgia—Atlanta—History. 4. Christmas decorations—Georgia—Atlanta—History. 5. Christmas trees—Georgia—Atlanta—History. 6. Christmas cookery—Georgia—Atlanta—Hsitory. 7. Atlanta (Ga.)—Social life and customs.
  GT4986.G4I76 2004
  394.2663'09758'231—dc22   2004016773

ISBN # 1-58818-099-9

10 9 8 7 6 5 4 3 2 1   First printing

To the late Frank Pallotta, whose rich imagination created Priscilla and the Rich's-Macy's Great Tree.

Contents

Rain or shine, sleet or snow, at the Porch household when it was time for Santa Claus, it was also time for the Pink Pig. All three of my children grew up with the Pink Pig as a big part of their holiday celebration.

One year, when Barbara was twelve, Phil was eight, and Leigh Ann was four, we found ourselves standing in line on the roof of the downtown Rich's, waiting for their turn to ride the beloved Pink Pig Flyer. The two older children were giggling with excitement, but little Leigh Ann was nervous about her upcoming ride—and openly suspicious. New adventures were not something she looked forward to. I knew a problem was brewing when she said, "Daddy, I want you to ride with me." Trying to pass it off as an impossible request, I laughingly said, "Daddy is too big, sweetheart, but I'll wait here while you ride." Tears were welling up in her eyes and, through pooched-out lips, she said, "I'm not riding anything if you don't." She was only four years old, but she spoke with the finality of a jury foreman.

The pig stopped on the platform and the assembled crowd began to board. The little seats were filling rapidly. I told Leigh Ann she needed to hurry. She repeated, "If you're not going, I'm not going."

That's when I made the biggest mistake of my life. I said, "O.K. Let's do it." She got into a car and I squeezed my six-foot-plus frame into a space made for an eight-year-old. It was almost too tight to sneeze.

When it was time to unload after the ride, everything in my body was numb. I was unable to move, let alone disembark the pig. A teenaged employee walked up to me and said, "Sir, you'll have to get off now." He seemed amazed to find a grown-up stuck inside the tiny car. I soon drew a crowd of his equally amazed co-workers who were finally able to pull me free.

I was standing there, trying to get some feeling back in my legs, when a smiling Leigh Ann looked up at me and said, "Daddy, let's do it again!"

I wish we had.

Ludlow Porch

Introduction

In 1953, the world marveled as Edmund Hillary and Tenzing Norgay became the first humans to crest the summit of Mount Everest, Francis Crick and James Watson discovered the double-helix structure of DNA, and Elizabeth II was crowned queen of England. But for the small fry of Atlanta there was only one truly noteworthy event of 1953: the debut of Priscilla the Pink Pig. Clicking and clacking along a track suspended from the high ceiling of the downtown Rich's Wonderland of Toys, the Pink Pig Flyer gave pint-sized riders the benefit of a bird's-eye view of a toy department that rivaled even Santa's workshop with its treasure trove of Slinkies and Erector sets, Betsey Wetsey dolls and Radio Flyers, Silly Putty and coonskin caps, paint-by-number kits and Lionel trains, and on and on and on. . . . The brainchild of Rich's executive Frank Pallotta, Priscilla immediately captured the hearts of Atlantans of all ages and began her reign, continuing to the present day, as the city's most beloved holiday tradition.

After thrilling at the extravagantly decorated Great Tree atop the Crystal Bridge that spanned Forsyth Street to connect the two sections of the flagship Rich's (a tradition begun in 1947), kids might visit Santa's Secret Shop with their list—no doubt twice-checked—of family members, teachers, friends, and even pets for whom they needed to find a gift. Giddy with allowance money or their parents' Rich's charge card, kids could shop among displays loaded with potential presents.

No day of Christmas shopping would be complete without a visit to Santa in his Igloo in the Sky on the roof of the Store for Homes. Five-feet-eight-inch, 225-pound Raymond D. Hicks, full-time Rich's shoe salesman and part-time Methodist preacher, served as in-house Santa beginning in 1953.

"Santa is a state of mind," mused Hicks in a 1963 article in magazine entitled "Ten Years in an Igloo. "He can be as real when you're forty as when you're six. The kids are always excited when they come to see me, of course . . . but a lot of the time, so are the mothers. You can tell."

"And you'd be surprised at how many grandmothers come to the store to see old Santa. I've held as many grandmothers on my knee as children. To me, they're all alike," he continued. "I don't care if it's Miss America . . . if she runs to my knee, she comes as a child."

To cap off the busy day, children might be treated to a sweet from one of Rich's Bake Shops or, if they promised to sit up straight and say "please" and "thank you," to lunch at Rich's Magnolia Room. The tearoom was as famous for its elegant décor and solicitous service as for its signature chicken pie, chicken amandine and frozen fruit salad, and nut pound cake.

After 1963, Saint Nick moved to Santa's Christmas Park on the Plaza Deck, between the Store for Homes and the Spring Street viaduct. There, according to Rich's newsletter, children were "greeted by a sight to gladden all hearts—an old-fashioned buggy ride behind beautiful prancing horses through a park of Christmas trees, a never-never ride through the winter country-side right in the heart of the city."

Also in the mid-sixties, Percival Pig joined his sister swine and the twins ran on the roof of the Five Points Rich's through a fantasy landscape of oversized candy canes and gumdrops, and alongside a menagerie of animals, both exotic and familiar. For twenty-five cents, the ride on the three-hundred-feet-long track averaged three-and-a-half minutes of pure magic. A favorite feature of those years was a petting zoo featuring Santa's Reindeer House.

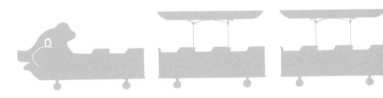

From 1991 to 1995, Priscilla joined the annual week-long Festival of Trees at the Georgia World Congress Center to help raise much-needed funds for her young friends at Egleston Children's Hospital. Still improbably pink and proudly porcine, Priscilla retired to the Atlanta History Center where she continued to make a yearly Yuletide appearance during the holiday Candlelight Tours of the center grounds as a part of the children's playscape.

Appropriate for a city whose seal bears the image of the mythological phoenix and the Latin motto *Resurgens* ("rising again"), it was only a matter of time before Atlanta's unofficial holiday mascot flew again. At age fifty, Priscilla got her second wind—and a makeover—for the 2003 holiday season, returning to delight kids young and old at the Rich's-Macy's at Lenox Square. Friends of Priscilla whose childhood rides had been captured on their parents' black-and-white Brownie Hawkeye filmed their kids'—even grandkids'—rides on digital camcorder. The unique, quirky tradition is now firmly set in the minds of Atlantans as the city's own, and for many it just wouldn't be the holiday season without a visit to Priscilla.

This celebration of Atlanta's unique and most beloved holiday tradition takes the form of a scrapbook. In it you'll find photos and remembrances from generations of Atlantans about Priscilla, the Great Tree, and everything that makes the

Befitting a city whose seal bears the image of the mythological phoenix, it was only a matter of time before Atlanta's divine swine flew again.

holiday special. Along the way, you'll find the story of how Priscilla came to be in "A Pig's Tale," written by Virginia Parker and illustrated by Sandy Culp; recipes (most of which you probably thought were lost forever) for some of the specialties of the Magnolia Room and Nathalie Dupree's tenure at the Rich's Cooking School; and "The Story of the Great Tree" penned by Marilyn Hill in 1964. And there are plenty of fun facts along the way. Finally, to continue this scrapbook as a keepsake of your own holiday memories, there's space in the back to write your own Pink Pig memories, and to save your own photos, stickers, and tickets.

Priscilla hopes that you enjoy this book as much as she's enjoyed her every Christmas in Atlanta and that you come back to reading and riding for generations to come!

 Patrick Allen

The Pink Pig:
Then & Now

The Pink Pig	then: 1953 Priscilla was Born	now: 2004 Priscilla Rides Again
Rich's-Macy's Stores in Atlanta	1	17
Metro Atlanta Population	508,000	3.5 million
Median Family Income	$4,242.00	$51,407.00
Minimum Hourly Wage	$0.75	$5.15
Avg. Home Price	$9,525.00	$218,875.00
Avg. Cost of a Dress	$17.98	$150.00
Avg. Cost of a Man's Suit	$40.90	$420.00
Avg. Cost of a Full-Size Car	$1,850.00	$20,000.00
Tuition at Emory College	$525.00	$28,940.00
Avg. Cost of Gasoline	$0.29/gal.	$1.59/gal.
Postage Stamp	$0.03 each	$0.37 each
On Television	*Dragnet*	*CSI*
At the Movies	*Peter Pan*	*Shrek 2*

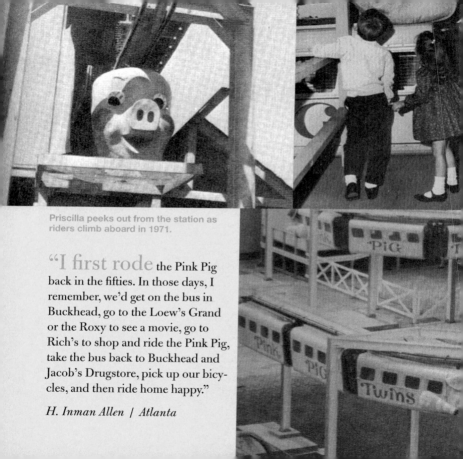

Priscilla peeks out from the station as riders climb aboard in 1971.

"I first rode the Pink Pig back in the fifties. In those days, I remember, we'd get on the bus in Buckhead, go to the Loew's Grand or the Roxy to see a movie, go to Rich's to shop and ride the Pink Pig, take the bus back to Buckhead and Jacob's Drugstore, pick up our bicycles, and then ride home happy."

H. Inman Allen | Atlanta

"The absolute magic of it. I was a child in the early 1960s. There was only one Rich's store then, a downtown palace of dreams. Mother loaded my sister and me into our family's squat black Ford and headed for the Atlanta skyline, a long drive from our farm south of the city. We arrived at the glorious Rich's store dressed in matching plaid jumpers and patent-leather shoes—my sister and me, that is, not Mom. Mom clutched her John Romaine purse.

That year, she'd let us ride the Pink Pig alone.

The pig hung from a rail in the ceiling of Rich's toy department like a smiling, porky ticket to fantasyland. I remember the smooth, exciting rumble as Priscilla glided along. I remember gaping out the tiny windows at the toys and Christmas decorations below. I remember the cinnamon-and-carpet scent, and I even remember the muted *whoosh* of the hydraulic tubes along the ceiling, carrying messages and invoices between the store's vast spaces.

Afterwards, Mom led us to a special shopping area, where she handed us a dollar or two then turned us over to motherly salesclerks. Spending a dime here and a quarter there, we shopped with a sense of grown-up pride. There, under the plaster gaze of the Pink Pig, the world seemed perfect."

Deborah Smith | Dahlonega, Ga.

The loveable Pink Pig Flyer high amongst the skyscrapers of Atlanta when it was located on the roof of Rich's downtown store beginning in the mid-1960s.

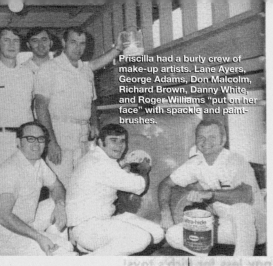

Priscilla had a burly crew of make-up artists. Lane Ayers, George Adams, Don Malcolm, Richard Brown, Danny White, and Roger Williams "put on her face" with spackle and paint-brushes.

"My cousin and I used to go to work with Daddy and my uncle at night, and while they worked, we rode the Pink Pig around the ceiling of Rich's toy store. Mr. Rich didn't mind."

Alford "Mike" Casey (1909–2003), whose father wired some of Rich's first Great Trees.

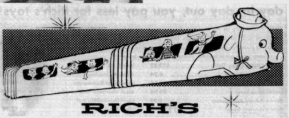

The Pink Pig Flyer blasts off in a 1950s newspaper ad.

"**Every year** we'd go downtown, ride the Pink Pig, gaze at the live reindeer and huge candy canes, and get the coveted 'I Rode the Pink Pig' sticker to wear to school. After the stickiness wore off, we'd resort to Elmer's glue, chewed-up gum, even leftover syrup from breakfast to keep it on our clothes."

Jan Butsch | Atlanta

Averell Johnson whispers her wish list to Santa in 1967.

A favorite part of the Pink Pig Park was a petting zoo featuring Santa's Reindeer House.

Breakfast with Santa was always a thrill.

"My sisters Angela *(center)* and Melanie *(right)* and I loved our yearly visit to Santa. I am five-and-a-half years old in this picture from 1967. We would ride the Pink Pig, see the Great Tree, look at the reindeer, and then we would visit Santa's Secret Shop, where we could buy presents for our family. It was such a great memory of my growing-up in Atlanta! As you can see, we have our Pink Pig stickers on our dresses!"

Robin Pruett Odom

21

Debbie Murrell finds cooking fun in a 1965 Kiddie Kitchen.

The Animal Zoo, 1966.

Stuart, Douglas, and Mark Kavanagh race Hot Wheels with their dad in 1968. The cars debuted that year—the sixteen different models cost fifty-nine cents each—and were an instant success.

Chris Burford is queen of the Wonderland of Toys, 1971.

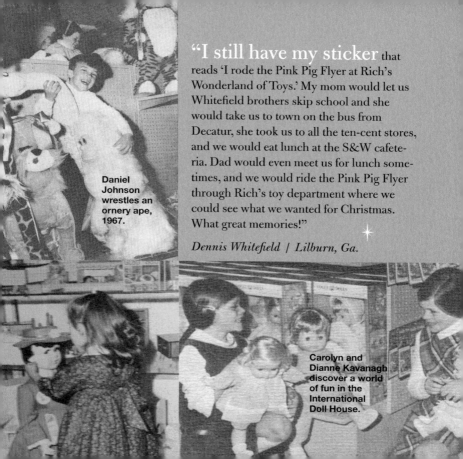

"I still have my sticker that reads 'I rode the Pink Pig Flyer at Rich's Wonderland of Toys.' My mom would let us Whitefield brothers skip school and she would take us to town on the bus from Decatur, she took us to all the ten-cent stores, and we would eat lunch at the S&W cafeteria. Dad would even meet us for lunch sometimes, and we would ride the Pink Pig Flyer through Rich's toy department where we could see what we wanted for Christmas. What great memories!"

Dennis Whitefield | Lilburn, Ga.

Daniel Johnson wrestles an ornery ape, 1967.

Carolyn and Dianne Kavanagh discover a world of fun in the International Doll House.

Tucked away on the fifth floor bridge of the downtown store was an enchanted and magical place—Santa's Secret Shop. NO PARENTS ALLOWED!

Edward Johnson knows that Laura King will keep his Christmas secrets, 1967.

Shhhh...!

Sales associate Lib Taylor helps a young customer find gifts in Santa's Secret Shop where prices ranged from fifty cents to three dollars in 1965.

"Santa's Secret Shop was magical.

High-school kids dressed as elves would pin a long white list to each child. On this list were the names of all people for whom he or she needed to get gifts. At the bottom of the list was a little pocket that held either an amount of money or a Rich's credit card. I was taken by the hand and lead into this magical orange-and-fuchsia, sparkly, lit-up world (after all it was the sixties!), kind of like a tunnel. Inside the tunnel were display tables with very reasonably priced items from the store. We would pick out an item and our elf would jot it down. When we were through, all the items would be waiting for us (wrapped, if memory serves) at the end of the journey. Even the paper shopping bag matched the scene, it was orange-and-fuchsia striped, read *Santa's Secret Shop,* and had a cartoon drawing of a little boy's face holding a finger to his mouth as if to shush you and not tell what was in the bag."

Louise Tate

25

Santa's Secret Shop, shown here in 1973, was begun in 1960 to cater to children ages three to twelve.

The Pink Pig Flyer at Christmas
1990, its last year downtown.

Luke Woodall, age
four, gets one of the
last pig's-eye views
of the downtown
skyline, 1990.

26

"My four-year-old daughter, Mae, has ridden the Pink Pig, and that was quite a moment for me, not when she was actually riding it, but when she talked about it so much afterward.

That is pretty much the moment I really understood that, while I myself am from California, I was raising a Southern daughter, and she's going to have this passel of memories and heritage to draw upon throughout her life that are so foreign from my own. Most parents understand in an abstract sense that their children are sovereign little entities with entire galaxies of personal wonderment in store for them, but still, stupidly, we're surprised when we realize that not all of those experiences will include us. In fact, it's possible very few will, and we are lucky for those. I'm very happy for my daughter's Southern-ness, having been sealed by her fascination with the Pink Pig, even if it marks the first of her many future memberships to clubs that can't include me."

Hollis Gillespie | Atlanta

Priscilla had a well-deserved spa treatment, courtesy of Custom Fiberglass Shop in Sugar Hill, Georgia, in November 1995. The following year, Carter Towing employee Danny Phelps gave her a lift to her new digs at the Atlanta History Center.

27

Year-old Samantha Katz has a play date with Priscilla *(left)* and Percival at the Annual Candlelight Tour of the Atlanta History Center in 1997. Samantha and mother Kym enjoyed choirs, folk musicians, and carolers stationed throughout the center as they toured the grounds.

"As a child, it was hard to imagine the holiday season without the Pink Pig. I can remember squeezing into the cars enclosed with the grates and embarking on a fanciful journey around the Great Tree. Seeing the huge decorations around the tremendous tree with downtown as the backdrop put the spirit into the season."

Maria Saporta | Atlanta

A new generation of riders enjoys the Pink Pig at the Lenox Square Rich's-Macy's in 2003. And the tradition continues.

A prettied-up Priscilla meets friends at the mall in 2003.

"Of *course* I remember riding the Pink Pig! It was a big deal back then to go downtown to Rich's at Christmas. My mother and I would get all dressed up (one wore a hat and gloves to shop back then) and we'd drive downtown from Decatur and be there when the doors opened. I remember the spearmint-flavored candy Christmas trees that were handed out after one's visit with Santa, and innumerable bottles of cologne I bought for my father at Santa's Secret Shop. I even remember the children's nursery with its built-in merry-go-round in the middle of the floor. The view from the Pink Pig of all the lights was stupendous. Christmas would never have come to Atlanta in my youth had Rich's and the Pink Pig not been there to bring it."

Betsy Dorminey | Athens, Ga.

29

The Holly men count down to the lighting of the Great Tree on Thanksgiving night, 1966.

The Great Tree is always a Georgia white pine, averages seventy feet tall, and is decorated with twelve hundred basketball-sized ornaments.

When the story is ended and the last choir has sung,

a switch is thrown and the big tree, subject of months of planning, hard work, and expense, suddenly blazes with light.

"Silent night, holy night," sing the choirs. And down in the street the crowd takes up the carol: "All is calm, all is bright . . ."

From the big tree a radiance reflects on the faces of children standing below in the darkness and sometimes it makes prisms of tears on the faces of grownups.

Christmas has officially begun in Atlanta.

Celestine Sibley / From Dear Store: An Affectionate Portrait of Rich's *(1967)*

At the annual lighting of the Great Tree, choirs accompanied longtime WSB radio announcer Bob Van Camp as he read the Scriptural account of Jesus' birth. A children's choir began the music from the lowest level of the bridge and then the music swept upward floor-by-floor. *(Left to right):* Clinton Burks, Bobbie Starks, and Ossie Addison, part of Rich's own Christmas choir, joined in the ceremony. "Silent Night" was always the final song.

"As a member of Rich's Teen Board from Decatur High School in 1960, I sold tickets for those who'd climb aboard. What a thrill! Christmas at Rich's was always beautiful but in 1960 it seemed especially lovely. Teen Board members dressed as elegant Madam Alexander dolls and shared our lookalike dolls with customers as we strolled through the Wonderland of Toys. The star of the show, however, was the Pink Pig Flyer and WE took turns selling her tickets!"

Susan Sellman Hamilton | *Decatur, Ga.*

Five Points businesses dimmed their lights and the city turned off the surrounding streetlights before the switch was flipped on the Great Tree each Thanksgiving night. The first Great Tree was lit in 1947 and the ceremony was televised for the first time in 1958 by WSB.

"Auntie Helen encouraged, coerced, cajoled, and insisted that four generations of Atlanta natives and their significant guests ride the Pink Pig. In 2003, our family celebrated with Atlanta the revival of this Christmas tradition. Nineteen strong—four generations ranging in age from seven months to sixty-five years—we had our picture taken with Priscilla. The photographer requested that our "ringleader" be moved to the first row, so Auntie Helen stood at the forefront—where she belongs."

Tami D. Kemberling | Fayetteville, Ga.

"I have happy memories of my family's trek from Marietta to Atlanta for shopping. At Christmas, that had to include a ride on the Pink Pig. Now, we did not have much money to do anything, but somehow we got to ride the Pig. We are a three-generation family of 'Piggers!'"

Rena Jarvis | Taylorsville, Ga

33

Celebrants crowded
Forsyth Street to sing
along with the choirs and
be dazzled by the lights.

"I first rode the pig in 1957 or '58, I think. We always shopped in Atlanta for Christmas and Easter. We would leave home before sunrise, wearing our pajamas, sitting in the back seat of the car with pillows and a quilt. Mother would wrap ham and a biscuit in waxed paper for us to eat when we got really awake. We would get dressed and be ready to shop. Oh how excited we were to eat all-day suckers and look at all of the store decorations. My mother had to touch and look at everything. By the end of the day, we were exhausted."

Connie Bryant Posey | Newnan, Ga.

"My husband and I took our daughter Mary Helen to ride Priscilla in 1979, when she was about eighteen months old. It was set up on the roof of the downtown Rich's, and there were various animals (I remember a deer and ducks or geese) in runs below. It was a cold, windy day. A man helped us into the cars, one for each of us. The cars were swinging back and forth, and you could see the ground, far below, miles and miles at least. The cars moved slowly around the rail, swinging out toward the edge of the building as they rounded the corners. Mary Helen loved it!"

Nancy DuPree | Tuscaloosa, Ala.

"Do I remember the Pink Pig? Yes, ma'am, I do. I remember the Pink Pig before there was Miss Piggie and Babe—yes, before pigs were cool!

One of my fondest childhood memories was the excitement at Christmas of going downtown to Rich's to the toy department. Riding the Pink Pig was a highlight of Christmas. We always had to wait in line with anticipation. It was so exciting when it was our turn—my sister and me—to get the chance to ride around looking down at the delights of the toy store."

Lane D. Sauser / Auburn, Ala.

"Oh my gosh, do I remember the Pink Pig. It wasn't Christmas until my brother and I rode Priscilla. It was such a magical time!"

Donna Gordon / Sharpsburg, Ga.

The Great Tree was lit at Underground Atlanta from 1991 to 1998 and white lights replaced the traditional multi-colored ones of previous years.

"Priscilla and I were both born the same year: 1953. Later, my mother would take my brother and me to Rich's to the toy department, where we would ride the Pink Pig as it soared over all the latest offerings for Christmas. Over the bicycles with the "banana" seats and chopper handlebars, the newest toys and best games, the Pink Pig carried us, and helped create dreams that only Santa Claus could make come true. The Pink Pig carried not only children, but dreams. What wonderful memories!"

Tom Jennings | Winder, Ga.

37

"Rich's was a mythical place during the holidays. On Thanksgiving night, family and friends would gather in the streets surrounding Rich's for Christmas carols and the lighting of the Great Tree. All three levels of the Crystal Bridge would illuminate as the tree's lights was turned on for the season. It was awesome.

The next day, my family would join the other shoppers looking for special gifts. My mind was on one thing—getting to the Pink Pig. The monorail traveled through animated storybook displays, similar to the windows in New York City. All of Mother Goose's friends were there: Humpty Dumpty, Cat 'n' Fiddle, Jack and the Bean Stalk, just to name a few. I remember one time when the monorail traveled over the toy department, and I had to hold my young brother by his suspenders as he reached out to point at the GI Joe display."

Joyce Dixon / Claxton, Ga.

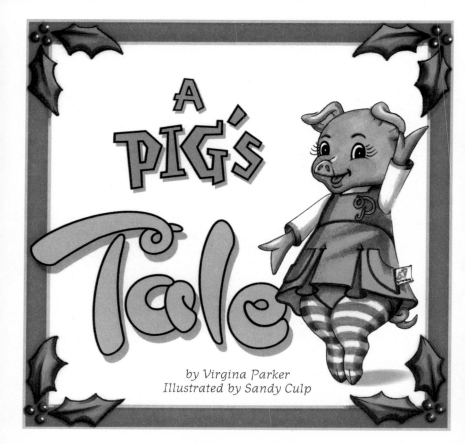

A PIG'S Tale

by Virgina Parker
Illustrated by Sandy Culp

nce upon a time there was a beautiful piglet as pink as bubble gum and twice as bouncy. She had intelligent eyes, a winsome smile, and her name was Priscilla. She lived with her mother, her father, and her two aunts in a big brick house on Hollyberry Street. And this is her story.

The morning of Thanksgiving, Priscilla bounded to the kitchen and gobbled up her biscuits and honey. Next to Christmas, Thanksgiving was Priscilla's favorite holiday and she practiced cleaning her plate and being grateful for weeks before the big day. Her family beamed with approval.

Her father gave Priscilla a big hug, and went to his job at the bank, looking dignified and important. Her mother put on her earrings, smiled at her reflection in the mirror, kissed Priscilla, and left for her job at the store.

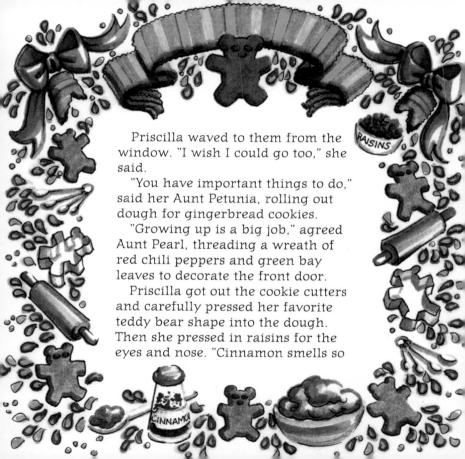

Priscilla waved to them from the window. "I wish I could go too," she said.

"You have important things to do," said her Aunt Petunia, rolling out dough for gingerbread cookies.

"Growing up is a big job," agreed Aunt Pearl, threading a wreath of red chili peppers and green bay leaves to decorate the front door.

Priscilla got out the cookie cutters and carefully pressed her favorite teddy bear shape into the dough. Then she pressed in raisins for the eyes and nose. "Cinnamon smells so

RAISINS

CINNAMON

good," she said sniffing happily. "When I grow up, maybe I'll be a baker." She popped a plump raisin into her mouth.

"Pigs in our family all love what they do, and do what they love," said Aunt Petunia.

"What do you think I should do?" asked Priscilla.

"You have to decide that for yourself," Aunt Pearl said. "But my advice is to follow your heart. What would you like to do?"

"Right now, I'd like to go and play with my friends!" said Priscilla promptly.

And she put on mittens and a muffler knitted by Aunt Pearl, filled her pockets with cookies made by Aunt Petunia, and off she skipped down Hollyberry Street.

Priscilla trotted straight to the playground. Everyone was talking about what they were bringing to this year's Thanksgiving feast.

"We're bringing grapes," said Francine Fox. "Super sweet."

"My mom is making her famous stew," said Blossom Possum, patting her tummy.

"Save some room for our hush puppies," greendog
said.

"We've saved up tin cans, string, and some paper," said
Gregory Goat. "You know, recycling."

Priscilla's mouth watered. She slid down the
slide, raced Blossom to the top of
the monkey bars, and took turns
pushing Francine on the swings
until they were both breathless.

"When I grow up, I'm going to be a ballerina," the fox said. She twirled gracefully on her tiptoes and curtseyed to an imaginary audience.

"Me too," said Priscilla. She spun around in a pirouette and fell flat on her curly pink tail. *Kerplunk!*

"Hey, Gregory," Priscilla asked, scrambling up. "What do you want to be?"

"I'm going to race motorcycles," said the goat, zipping by on his skateboard. *"Vroooom!"*

"I love going fast," said Priscilla, huffing and puffing as she ran after him.

"I'm going to be an artist," Blossom said, coloring a star with sidewalk chalk.

"Why, my favorite color is pink," said Priscilla, stopping to admire the possum's drawing. *Crunch* went the chalk under Priscilla's trotter.

"Sorry," said Blossom, "I'm all out of pink."

"Some day I'll be the leader of a band," said greendog, doing imaginary drumrolls. "And I'll march in the Christmas parade down Peachtree Street."

"I could be a majorette," said Priscilla. "Everyone loves a parade." And she pranced a few high-stepping paces before she tripped and flipped over sideways. *Bam!*

Gregory and greendog helped pull Priscilla to her feet. She was extra pink with embarrassment and her eyes filled with tears. It was a sad little pig who walked slowly home.

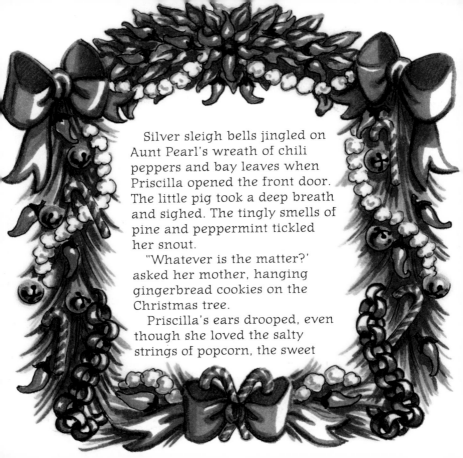

Silver sleigh bells jingled on Aunt Pearl's wreath of chili peppers and bay leaves when Priscilla opened the front door. The little pig took a deep breath and sighed. The tingly smells of pine and peppermint tickled her snout.

"Whatever is the matter?" asked her mother, hanging gingerbread cookies on the Christmas tree.

Priscilla's ears drooped, even though she loved the salty strings of popcorn, the sweet

candy canes, and the friendly smell of construction paper and paste from the paper chains she had made all by herself.

She told her mother about her morning at the playground. "All my friends know what they want to be," the little pig wailed mournfully, "except me." A tear trickled down her snout.

"I think you should talk to your grandmother. She'll have an idea or two," her mother said, calmly tying cookies to the branches.

"When you were a piglet, what did you want to do when you grew up?" Priscilla said, snuffling a little. High on top of the tree, a golden star winked. The mysterious bundles, shopping bags, and packages she'd seen being carried into the house for weeks had turned into temptingly wrapped gifts beneath the Christmas tree.

Her mother sat down in her rocking chair, held out her arms, and Priscilla climbed into her lap. Her mother smiled down at her. "I wanted to have fun, move in friendly circles, and leave the world a little happier than I found it."

"And do you?" Priscilla asked, yawning and rubbing her eyes.

"Oh yes," her mother said and kissed the tip of Priscilla's ear. "And I'll tell you a secret. It's not just about what you want. It's about what you have to give."

"But I can't dance, or draw, or skate, or anything." Priscilla protested sleepily and yawned again.

"I know a little pig who needs a nap," her mother said and before she could deny it, Priscilla fell fast asleep and dreamed of candied yams with marshmallows on top.

nock knock knock. The
pig family tapped on
Grandmother's door.
"Right on time,"
cried Grandmother,
opening the door wide.
The Thanksgiving table was piled
high with biscuits hot from the
oven, honey-glazed carrots, cran-
berry sauce, buttered broccoli,
green beans, corn on the cob, and
candied yams. There were pecan
and pumpkin pies, yellow cake
with chocolate frosting and

Priscilla's favorite, banana pudding topped with swirly meringue.

As her friends Blossom, greendog, Gregory, and Francine arrived, Priscilla ran back and forth until the hall closet was filled with coats, and the sideboard was covered in casserole dishes.

Finally everyone was gathered around the table. As platters and bowls began to circle and plates began to fill, Priscilla took a deep breath.

"Grandmother, how did you decide what to do when you grew up?" she asked in a small voice.

"Why, that is one of my favorite stories," Grandmother said, as she passed the mashed potatoes. "Would you like me to tell you?"

"Oh yes!" said Priscilla.

"When I was young and still new to the world," Grandmother began, "I left the farm and traveled to Atlanta to make my fortune."

"That was so brave," said Priscilla.

"I like to try things," Grandmother said modestly.

"Me too," said Priscilla, her eyes shining. "What happened next?"

"A taxi driver asked me where I was going. I said *'to be the richest pig,'* but he heard *'Rich's pig.'* Before I knew it I was giving rides to children. And what good times we had," Grandmother said with a twinkle in her eye. "Every year I met new friends and old ones returned."

"Everyone knew her," Priscilla's father said proudly. "They called her the Pink Pig."

"I found out making children happy day in and day out is a very rich life," Grandmother smiled at Priscilla. "And when you love what you do, work is a pleasure."

"That's brilliant," Priscilla cried, bouncing in her chair—*boing boing boing*—with enthusiasm.

"When it was time for me to retire, I thought that chapter in my life was closed. Then your mother accepted the job. That was the proudest day of my life," Grandmother beamed.

Priscilla's mother blushed with pleasure.

"That's what I want to do," Priscilla said, jumping to her feet. *Crash!* Her chair toppled over backwards and—*waaaap!*—she tumbled over sideways. "Oh no. How could I ever give rides?" the little pig wailed.

Suddenly Blossom said, "You're a very nice shade of pink."

"You think so?" Priscilla brightened.

"And you're definitely friendly," greendog added. "You got that covered."

"That's true," Priscilla agreed.

"I can help you with your moves," said Gregory. "You'll get up to speed in no time."

Priscilla scrambled upright. "Really?"

"I'll help you with turns. All you need is a little practice," said Francine.

"Most important of all," Grandmother said, "you are willing to try."

"Oh yes," Priscilla said, her ears at a jaunty angle. "Thank you, thank you all." She looked around the table feeling glad and grateful with all her heart.

"Now for the feast," Grandmother sang out, and everyone cheered.

"Hooray!" cried Priscilla. And she knew this was the very best holiday ever.

Family sticks by you through thick and through thin
Cheers you on to the finish and applauds when you win.
The thing to know is, you're not on your own.
We can do together what we can't do alone.
Here's another clue that just might hold the key
Do what you love and you'll always be happy.

The End

61

The Story of the Great Tree

by Marilyn Hill

Once upon a time there was a great big forest on the side of a great big hill.

And way at the top beyond the great big forest, there grew a little tree.

All the other trees whispered and rustled together

And talked of the time when they'd grow tall and of the things they wanted to be.

But the little tree stood all alone, at the top of the great big hill,

And his only friend was a far-away star that danced in the great big sky.

At night when the other trees were murmuring sleepily among themselves,

The little tree sadly drooped his branches and watched the star dance by.

One day the merry woodcutters came to the side of the
great big hill
And the little tree's heart
leapt high with joy and
he thought,
"At last they will take me to
where the buzz saw
sings, to be made into
exciting things
Like houses and tables
and garden swings—and
even children's toys!"
But the little tree was too
far away on top of the
great big hill.

So the woodcutters felled all the other trees, then
hurried back to the mill.
The little tree grew sadder and sadder as he watched
them disappear.
And as twilight fell he drooped his head—and wept an
evergreen tear.

67

COME to the LIGHTING OF THE GREAT TREE

Suddenly the star shone bright in the
sky over the top of the big hill,
But the little tree only glanced at his
friend and sighed, "I'm up here still!
No one will climb this great big hill
to come and chop me down,
And I'll never be exciting things,
like dollhouses and garden swings
. . . much less children's toys!"
Far, far away the bright star twin-
kled and said, "Don't cry little
tree.
You must grow taller and
straighter for then you will
gladden the hearts of men!"
"Gladden the hearts of men?" said
the tree.
"Yes," said the star, "you wait and
see!"

Now at the same time there
was a great big store in the
middle of a great big town.
At the very heart of this great
big store, there was a great
big man.
The store was fine and modern
and busy, and it bustled the
whole year round
With people buying and people
selling, and the man was
happy with the way things
ran,
Until one day he called together
his chiefs and advisors and
said, "It's Christmas-time!"
"Now right at the top of this
great big store in the heart of
this great big town,
I want us to have the most
beautiful tree that anyone's
ever found."

A 1950s postcard shows the Great
Tree atop the Crystal Bridge linking
Rich's main store with the Store for
Homes.

69

**℃hristmas as we see it
at Rich's for 1955**

Unforgettable: The traditional "Lighting of the Great Tree"

Nostalgic: The scenes depicting familiar Christmas Carols
for ledges and windows

Fun: The many exciting Christmas shops, the Doll
House, the Grandmother's Shop, the For-Men-Only Shop, etc.

Successful: With wide assortments of everything that
this may be the best Christmas yet

*All in all, it looks like a **Wonderful Christmas** at Rich's.*

"A tree?" cried the chiefs and advisors.
"A tree!" said the man again. "A tree with a heart, a
tree that was born to gladden the hearts of men."
As the chiefs and advisors bustled all around, and they
searched and they looked and they knocked each
other down to find a tree.

Then many weeks later they all
    came back to the office of the
    great big man,
And each had a tree that was the
    very best he'd seen since the
    search began.
"Here is a tree imported from
    France, by a designer of world-
    wide fame.
It's chic! It's smart! It's the latest
    thing! And you can't pronounce
    the name!"
"And here is a tree that's the latest
    in science—a fantastic ATOMIC
    tree,
The nuclear composition of which
    has baffled the finest phy-si-
    cists!"

"... the lighting of the great tree marks the official beginning
of Christmas!"

The Atlanta Constitution
Nov. 26, 1952

Rich's lighted a Christmas tree and for an instant Atlanta's heart stood still,
for it was more than the lighting of a department store Christmas tree. It was a
moment of searching and savoring the pure magic of Christmas. Eighty thousand
people were there when the tree was lit and in Atlanta the Christmas season officially began."

RICH'S
A Southern Institution Since 1867

Yes, they all had trees, both
old and new, and a tree
by Cartier,
But the man only looked
and shook his head, and
waved them all away.
"You've missed the point,
the whole idea," said the
man, "for none of you
has found
A tree with a heart, a tree
that was born to glad-
den the hearts of men."

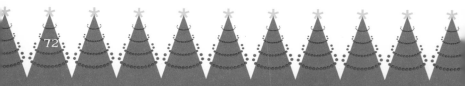

72

So the chiefs and advisors gathered their trees and
    went back to look some more.
And the great big man sat all alone at the top of the
    great big store.
"I must get a tree," he said to himself, "and I'll find it
    myself instead. But I don't know where to begin to
    look."

And as night came on, he suddenly saw, where he'd
    never seen one before,
A bright star dancing right outside, far above the great
    big store.
"What a bright shining star," thought the great big
    man, and what a lovely night I see.
I think I shall go for a walk by myself—and perhaps I
    shall find a tree!"
So he walked and he walked through the great big
    town, and then the countryside until
After walking even more he found himself at the foot
    of the great big hill.

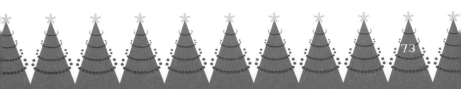

And there, by the light of the bright dancing star he
  looked—and then looked again!
For there was the tree, the little tree that had grown all
  alone as the years went by
Till its branches spread wide as a generous heart, and
  its top made friends with the sky.
The tree that was born to gladden the hearts of men!

"The tree! The tree!" cried the great big man and he
  danced and jumped up and down,
And he hurried back as fast as he could to the heart of
  the great big town.
Next day there came from the great big store in the
  heart of the great big town
All sorts of experts with experts' machines sure to
  bring the great tree down.
And they measured and discussed, and they argued
  and they fussed and felled the tree.
At last the tree was safely installed at the top of the
  great big store
And as he looked down he saw such sights as he'd
  never seen before!

And while he was looking
some pixies came with
boxes of wondrous things.
Balls and stars and cones
and tinsel and colored
lights on strings!
All day they worked and
matched and perfected
Trimming the tree with all
the colors and the shapes
and designs they'd
Softly the night began to
fall over the heart of the
great big town.
And down in the streets
the people gathered and
talked and milled around,
Till they heard the children begin
to sing in voices so true and clear
The songs that children have sung
and loved year after shining year.

In a 1961 cover story, *Time* declared that the "famed pageant at Rich's department store, with its lighted tree and massed choirs, sets the season's stage for the South."

Then slowly other voices joined in the glorious swell of
    sound,
And the great tree's heart nearly burst through his
    trunk with the new joy he'd found.
He saw the lifted faces below him so warm and loving
    and bright
And he stretched his branches out to them all—and
    exploded into light!
The great big man heaved a sigh of joy, and the lights
    on the tree burned brightly,
And if you'd looked very closely you'd have seen a star
    wink ever so slightly.

Windows made in 1967 to commemorate Rich's centennial anniversary are used at the Lenox Square Rich's-Macy's, where the Great Tree has been lit since 1999. The windows were crafted in Decatur by Lorenz Stained Glass.

RICH'S
MEN'S STORE

RICH'S
MEN'S STORE

RICH'S
MEN'S STORE

The Roots of the Rich's-Macy's
Great Tree

1947:
The first Great Tree, a twenty-feet tall cedar grown in College Park, Georgia, was lit.

1947-1988:
The Great Tree stood atop the Crystal Bridge over Forsyth Street spanning the main store and Rich's Store for Homes. Nearby businesses dimmed their lights and the city blacked out surrounding streetlights.

1958:
The Thanksgiving night lighting of the Great Tree is televised for the first time, on WSB-TV.

1991-1998:
The Great Tree is lit at Underground Atlanta. White lights replace the multi-colored lights used in previous years.

1999-present:
The Lenox Square flagship Rich's-Macy's hosts the lighting of the Great Tree. Lenox Square turns out its lights and the crowd is given balloons to release when the tree lights up.

Didja Know
the Great Tree...?

is always a Georgia white pine from right here in the Peach State
averages thirty-five feet around at the lowest branches, seventy feet
tall, twenty-five to thirty-five years old, and weighs an average of
sixteen thousand pounds fully decorated + drinks a mixture of two
hundred aspirins dissolved in three hundred gallons of water per day
to maintain its freshness ● is decorated with twelve hundred
basketball-sized ornaments, sixty two-and-a-half-feet tall teddy bears,
fifty flashing strobe lights, and three hundred internally lit ornaments
is electrified with more than eight miles of circuit wiring + is topped
with a spectacular, seven-feet tall, six-point star with seven hundred
lights + requires a decorating crew of eight people working for twenty-
one days and a lighting crew of ten working seven days + has a stand
and supports designed to weather hurricane-level storms + is
decorated sixty two-and-a-half-feet tall teddy bears which were added
in 2002, the hundredth anniversary of the teddy bear ● is recycled into
mulch for use at the Chattahoochee Nature Center ● was viewed by
over 2.2 million people in 2004 ● is always lit Thanksgiving Night,
accompanied by song and fireworks, beginning Christmas in Atlanta

79

Recipes

Once upon a time, visitors to the downtown Rich's might ride the Pink Pig, marvel at the Great Tree, and shop the Wonderland of Toys and Book Shop, before heading for lunch at the Magnolia Room or a quick snack at one of Rich's Bake Shops. With its light orange-and-green décor and hushed service, the tea room was an icon of white-gloved gentility from its opening in the 1940s until its closing in 1991. The in-store bakeries and candy kitchens with their Rich Bits and party mints likewise satisfied the sweet-tooths of generations of Atlantans. In 1972, Cordon Blue chef Nathalie Dupree began the Rich's Cooking School to rave reviews and went on to teach over 10,000 students. Her first cookbook, *Let's Entertain,* was a collection of recipes from the school. Following are some classic dishes—both savory and sweet—from the kitchens of the Magnolia Room, Rich's Bake Shops, and Dupree's classes.

Cheese Straws

From Magnolia Room Executive Chef
John Van Dyke

2 cups freshly shredded sharp Cheddar cheese
1/3 cup freshly grated imported Parmesan cheese
1 teaspoon cayenne pepper (or to taste)
Dash of kosher salt
1 (17-1/2-ounce) box (2 sheets) puff pastry
2 tablespoons unsalted butter, softened

Preheat oven to 425°F.

Mix together cheeses, pepper, and salt. Spread one sheet of puff pastry with butter. Spread with cheese mixture. Place second pastry sheet on top. Press ends of pastry sheet together. With a rolling pin, roll out to 1/4-inch thickness, about 15-by-15 inches. Cut across in 1-inch wide ribbons. Cut in half again. Twist each piece. Bake on lightly greased cookie sheet for 3 to 5 minutes or until puffed and lightly browned. Cool completely on a wire rack.

Yields 3 dozen.

Chicken Pie

Pastry:
- 3 cups sifted all-purpose flour
- 3/4 teaspoon kosher salt
- 3/4 cup (1-1/2 sticks) chilled unsalted butter, cut into small pieces
- 4-1/2 tablespoons chilled vegetable shortening, cut into small pieces
- 6 tablespoons (approximately) ice water
- 1 large whole egg, beaten

Filling:
- 1 stewing chicken (about 4 pounds), boiled
- 1 cup diced carrots, cooked
- 1 cup English peas, cooked
- 1/4 cup unsalted butter
- 1/4 cup sifted all-purpose flour
- 1 quart chicken stock, seasoned to taste with salt and freshly ground white pepper

To prepare pastry: Blend flour and salt in food processor. Add butter and shortening and pulse, until mixture resembles coarse meal. Add 4 tablespoons water and pulse. Add enough additional water by tablespoonfuls to form moist clumps. Gather dough into a ball; flatten into a disk. Wrap in plastic and chill until cold, at least 1 hour or up to 1 day.

To prepare filling: Strip chicken meat from the bones. Cut into 1-inch pieces. Place layers of chicken and vegetables in individual casseroles.

Melt butter in a saucepan over low heat. Blend in flour; cook and stir for 3 or 4 minutes. Slowly stir in the seasoned chicken stock. Raise heat slightly; simmer and stir with a whisk until thickened and bubbly.

To assemble pies: Preheat oven to 400°F. Cover chicken and vegetables with the sauce.

Roll out dough on lightly floured surface to 1/8-inch thickness. Cut out 6 rounds, each measuring 1/2 to 1 inches larger in diameter than casseroles, gathering dough and re-rolling as necessary. Lay pastry rounds atop filled casseroles. Firmly press the overhang to adhere to top rim of dish. Trim excess dough. Cut slits in dough for steam to escape. Brush crusts with beaten egg.

Bake 30 minutes on a parchment- or foil-lined cookie sheet in preheated oven until pies are bubbly and crust is crisp and lightly brown. Serve warm.

Yields 6 servings.

Chicken Salad Amandine with Frozen Fruit Salad

*This Magnolia Room specialty was a longtime,
year-round favorite of the Ladies Who Lunched.*

Chicken salad:
3-1/2 pounds chicken breasts
Salt to taste
6 ribs celery, diced
1/2 cup pickle relish, well drained
1-1/2 teaspoons freshly ground white pepper
2 cups mayonnaise
1/2 cup sliced, toasted almonds

Frozen fruit salad:
8 ounces cream cheese, softened
1/2 cup confectioners' sugar
1/3 cup mayonnaise
2 teaspoons pure vanilla extract
1 (8-3/4-ounce) can sliced peaches, well drained
1/2 cup maraschino cherry halves, well drained
1 (30-ounce) can fruit cocktail, well drained
1 (6-1/2-ounce) can crushed pineapple, well drained
2 cups miniature marshmallows
1/2 cup whipping cream, whipped
Red or yellow food coloring (optional)
Whipped cream for garnish (optional)

For chicken salad: Boil chicken breasts in lightly salted water until meat is tender. Reserve stock for future use. Let chicken cool. Separate meat from bones and skin; leave chicken in medium-size strips.

Fold celery, pickle relish, and pepper into mayonnaise. Fold chicken into mayonnaise mixture. Cover and refrigerate until serving. Garnish with almond slices.

For fruit salad: Combine cream cheese and confectioners' sugar in a medium bowl using a hand mixer on medium speed; blend in mayonnaise. Add vanilla extract. Gently fold in fruit and marshmallows by hand. Gently fold whipped cream into fruit mixture. Add food coloring, if desired. Ladle into 12 large soufflé cups or paper muffin liners. Freeze immediately for at least three hours. Defrost 15 minutes before serving. Do not allow to get soft. Remove soufflé cups or muffin liners before serving. Garnish with additional whipped cream, if desired.

Yields 12 servings.

Georgia Pecan Pie

3 large whole eggs
2 tablespoons unsalted butter, melted
2 tablespoons all-purpose flour
1/4 teaspoon pure vanilla extract
1/4 teaspoon salt
1/2 cup granulated sugar
1-1/2 cups dark corn syrup
1-1/2 cups broken pecans
1 unbaked 9-inch pie shell
Sweetened whipped cream for garnish (optional)
Finely chopped toasted pecans for garnish (optional)

Preheat oven to 425°F.

Beat eggs in a large bowl, then blend in butter, flour, vanilla, salt, sugar, and corn syrup. Sprinkle pecans over bottom of unbaked pie shell. Gently pour syrup mixture over pecans and bake at 425°F for 10 minutes. Reduce heat to 325°F and bake for 30 additional minutes. Cool completely on a wire rack. Garnish with whipped cream and pecans, if desired.

Yields 8 servings.

Pecan Cream Torte

1-1/2 cups firmly packed
   dark brown sugar
1 cup cake crumbs
1/2 cup vegetable shortening
2 tablespoons all-purpose
   flour
1/2 teaspoon baking powder
5 large eggs, separated

1-1/2 cups finely chopped
   pecans
1 pint whipped cream,
   sweetened and whipped
Finely chopped toasted
   pecans for garnish
   (optional)

Preheat oven to 350°F. Grease two 9-inch layer cake pans;
line the bottoms with greased parchment or wax paper.

Cream sugar, crumbs, shortening, flour, and baking
powder until smooth. Add egg yolks and pecans. Mix until
smooth. Whip the whites until they hold a soft peak and
fold into batter.

Pour batter into prepared pans. Bake in preheated oven
for 20 to 25 minutes or until a cake tester or toothpick
stuck into the middle of the torte comes out clean. Do not
overbake. Remove from pans and cool completely on a
wire rack. Frost tops of cooled layers with whipped cream
and stack one layer atop the other; garnish edge with
pecans, if desired.

Yields 6 to 8 servings.

Nut Poundcake

3-3/4 cups cake flour
1 teaspoon salt
1/4 cup powdered milk
1-1/4 cups plus 1 tablespoon
  unsalted butter
2-1/4 cups granulated sugar
1 cup minus 2 tablespoons
  water

8 large eggs
1 teaspoon pure vanilla extract
2 cups pecan pieces
Sweetened whipped cream
  for garnish (optional)
Finely chopped toasted
  pecans for garnish
  (optional)

Preheat oven to 375°F. Grease and flour a large tube pan; set aside.

In a medium mixing bowl, sift together the flour, salt, and powdered milk. In large bowl using an electric mixer, cream the butter and sugar together about 3 minutes. Add the dry ingredients and mix until just combined. Add water and beat on medium speed for 6 minutes. Add the eggs and beat on medium speed for 3 minutes. Stir in the vanilla extract. Fold in the pecan pieces. Pour into prepared pan and bake 40 minutes, or until a cake tester or toothpick stuck into the middle of the cake comes out clean.

Cool in pan on wire rack for 10 minutes; remove from pan and cool completely on wire rack. Garnish with whipped cream and pecans, if desired.

Yields 16 servings

Christmas Fruit Candy

A Nathalie Dupree holiday favorite.

3 cups granulated sugar
1 cup light corn syrup
1-1/2 cups heavy cream
1/4 teaspoon salt
1 teaspoon pure vanilla extract
8 ounces pecan halves
8 ounces walnut halves
8 ounces candied cherries
8 ounces diced candied pineapple

Grease a 9"-inch loaf pan. Mix sugar, corn syrup, cream, and salt in a heavy-bottom saucepan, bring to a boil, and cook without stirring until the mixture reaches 236°F on a candy thermometer, or until a small amount of the mixture dropped into very cold water forms a soft ball that flattens when removed from water.

Remove from heat and let stand 5 minutes. Add vanilla extract and beat until slightly thick. Add nuts and fruit and mix well. Pack firmly into prepared pan, let stand overnight.

Cut into thick slices, then into batons.

Yields 4-1/2 pounds.

Gateau d'Ananas

A beloved Christmas cake from renowned chef and
James Beard Award winner Nathalie Dupree,
founder of the Rich's Cooking School in 1972.

3 ounces all-purpose flour
Pinch salt
3 large whole eggs
2-3 tablespoons diced
 pineapple
8 thin slices pineapple
4 tablespoons apricot jelly

1/4 pint whipping cream,
 whipped and flavored with
 granulated sugar, pure
 vanilla extract, and kirsch
 to taste
Candied cherries and
 angelica (for decoration)

Preheat oven to 350°F. Oil a 9-inch cake pan. Flour, then
sprinkle lightly with sugar.

Sift together flour and salt in a small bowl. Whisk
together eggs and sugar in a heavy-bottom saucepan over
gentle heat until thick and mousse-like; remove from heat
and continue whisking until mixture has cooled.

Quickly fold the flour mixture into the cooled egg mixture
and turn into the prepared pan. Bake in preheated oven for
15-20 minutes, or until a cake tester or toothpick stuck in the
middle of the cake comes out clean. Turn onto a wire rack to
cool completely.

Fold diced pineapple into whipped cream. Split the cooled cake into two layers. Spread whipped cream between layers and stack one atop the other. Transfer to serving plate.

Melt the apricot jelly in a heavy-bottom saucepan over gentle heat and brush over the cake. Arrange slices of pineapple, cherries, and angelica on top.

Yields 6 to 8 servings.

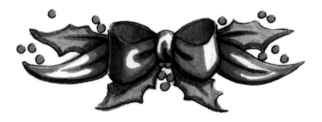

My Pink Pig Memories

I rode the Pink Pig with _____

_____

on _____
           month   day   year

My favorite part was _____

_____

_____

_____

_____

I can't wait till next year!

My Sticker

Illustration Credits

Unless otherwise noted below, all illustrations are from the Rich's-Macy's archives. © Rich's-Macy's, a division of Federated Department Stores, Inc. All rights reserved.

[19] Courtesy of Jeff Jensen/U.S. General Services Administration
[18, 58, 60, 81] © *Atlanta Journal-Constitution*
[21 *(bottom)*]Courtesy of Robin Pruett Odom. All rights reserved.
[26-45, 86-91] Sandy Culp. © 2004 by Rich's-Macy's Inc. All rights reserved.
[59] Laura Noel/*Atlanta-Journal Constitution* © *Atlanta Journal-Constitution.* All rights reserved.
[61] Courtesy of Children's Healthcare of Atlanta. All rights reserved.
[65, 78, 82, 76] Courtesy of the Atlanta History Center, James G. Kenan Research Center. All rights reserved.
[71] Courtesy of the Hargrett Rare Book and Manuscript Library, University of Georgia Libraries.

Acknowledgments

Several generations of Atlantans and Georgians, the venerable Ludlow Porch not the least among them, contributed remembrances and photographs to this family album—the generosity and enthusiasm of Mr. Porch and his fellow Flyer fans is appreciated.

Special thanks must go to Susan Hancock, Virginia Parker, Marla C. Shavin, and Kyla Tilton at Rich's-Macy's, and Patrick Allen, Anne Richmond Boston, and Thomas Payton at Hill Street Press. Illustrator Sandy Culp deserves kudos for her excellent original illustrations and decorative borders, as do Pam Prouty and the photo research staff at the *Atlanta Journal-Constitution* for their assistance with archival photos.

Recipes in this book are reprinted or adapted from the *Atlanta Journal-Constitution [Rich's Nut Poundcake, Rich's Cheese Straws]*, Earlyne S. Levitas' *Secrets from Atlanta's Best Kitchens* (Charleston, S.C.: Walker, Evans & Cogswell Co., 1972) [Chicken Pie and Pecan Cream Torte], and *Chef's Secrets from Great Restaurants in Georgia* (Atlanta: Marmac Publishing Co., 1983) [Chicken Salad Amandine with Frozen Fruit Salad]. Many thanks to Susan Puckett and Ginny Everett at the *AJC* for their help in locating these original sources.

The editor appreciates the assistance of Atlanta History Center curator of urban and regional history Don Rooney and archivist Michael Rose, as well as that of the staff of the AHC's James G. Kenan Research Center. U.S. General Services Administration historic preservation and fine arts specialist Jeffrey M. Jensen and Children's Healthcare of Atlanta's Laura Prediletto were kind to provide photo research assistance. The Hargrett Rare Book and Manuscript Library at the University of Georgia, the Special Collections Department at the Pullen Library at Georgia State University, and the Library of Congress also provided much-appreciated assistance. Marshall Akers deserves thanks for his time and expertise.